SUPER
SANDCASTLE™
Super Simple Crafts

SUPER SIMPLE
Masks

WITHDRAWN

Fun and Easy-to-Make
Crafts for Kids

Karen Latchana Kenney

Consulting Editor, Diane Craig, M.A./Reading Specialist

ABDO
Publishing Company

Published by ABDO Publishing Company, 8000 West 78th Street, Edina, Minnesota 55439.
Copyright © 2010 by Abdo Consulting Group, Inc. International copyrights reserved in all
countries. No part of this book may be reproduced in any form without written permission from
the publisher. Super SandCastle™ is a trademark and logo of ABDO Publishing Company.

Printed in the United States.

Editor: Liz Salzmann
Content Developer: Nancy Tuminelly
Cover and Interior Design and Production: Oona Gaarder-Juntti, Mighty Media
Photo Credits: Colleen Dolphin, Shutterstock
Activity Production: Oona Gaarder-Juntti

The following manufacturers/names appearing in this book are trademarks:
Elmer's® Glue-All™, Reynolds® Cut-Rite® Waxed Paper, Target® Aluminum Foil,
Office Depot® Posterboard, Crayola® Washable Glitter Glue

Library of Congress Cataloging-in-Publication Data

Kenney, Karen Latchana.
 Super simple masks : fun and easy-to-make crafts for kids / Karen Latchana Kenney.
   p. cm. -- (Super simple crafts)
 ISBN 978-1-60453-627-0
 1. Mask making--Juvenile literature. I. Title.

TT898.K455 2010
731'.75--dc22
                        2009000357

Super SandCastle™ books are created by a team of professional educators, reading
specialists, and content developers around five essential components—phonemic awareness,
phonics, vocabulary, text comprehension, and fluency—to assist young readers as they develop
reading skills and strategies and increase their general knowledge. All books are written,
reviewed, and leveled for guided reading, early reading intervention, and Accelerated Reader®
programs for use in shared, guided, and independent reading and writing activities to support a
balanced approach to literacy instruction.

To Adult Helpers

Making a mask is fun and simple to do. Glue, markers, and paint
will be used in some activities. Make sure kids protect their clothes
and work surfaces before starting.

Table of Contents

Symbols

Look for this symbol in this book.

 Adult Help. Get help! You will
need help from an adult.

Making Masks!

Want to look like a lion or a butterfly? You can do it! Just try making a mask. It's simple! Create it from a paper plate or an egg carton. Then put it on! Try some or all of the masks in this book. It's up to you! From start to finish, making super simple masks is fun to do!

Tools and Supplies

Here are many of the things you will need to do the **projects** in this book. You can find them online or at your local craft store.

craft foam

construction paper

paintbrushes

paper bags

acrylic paint

sequins

felt

yarn

egg carton

duct tape

paper streamers

feathers

scissors

furry fabric

silver cupcake liners

Styrofoam balls

plastic party mask

bucket

aluminum foil

paper raffia

thick paper plates

hole punch

poster board

paint stirring stick

glue

glitter glue

wax paper

elastic cord

pipe cleaners

googly eyes

5

Jungle Animals

You'll go wild for these paper plate masks!

Supply List

- thick paper plates
- pencil
- scissors
- acrylic paint
- paintbrush
- craft foam or construction paper
- stapler
- hole punch
- elastic cord
- yarn (yellow)
- paper raffia (yellow or orange)
- glue
- paint stirring stick
- tape

Panda

1 Hold a paper plate to your face. Have an adult draw around where your eyes and mouth are. Have an adult help cut out the eye and mouth holes.

2 Paint two big black circles around the eye holes. Paint a small black nose under the eyes. Outline the mouth with black. Let the paint dry.

3 Use black foam or construction paper for the ears. Cut out two circles. **Staple** the circles to the rim of the plate above the eyes.

4 Punch a hole on each side of the plate. Cut a piece of elastic cord. It should reach around the back of your head. Tie one end of the cord to each hole.

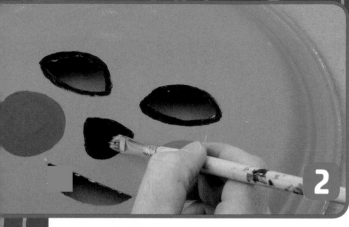

Lion

1 Hold a paper plate to your face. Have an adult draw around where your eyes and mouth are. Have an adult help cut out the eye and mouth holes.

2 Paint the plate orange. Outline the eyes with black. Paint two brown circles for the cheeks. Add a black upside-down triangle for the nose. Let the paint dry.

3 Use orange foam or construction paper to make the ears. Cut out two circles. **Staple** them to the rim of the plate.

4 Cut yellow yarn into 3-inch (8-cm) pieces. Glue them to the back of the plate around the rim. Add shorter pieces of raffia. Glue on raffia **whiskers**.

5 Punch a hole on each side of the plate. Cut a piece of elastic cord. It should reach around the back of your head. Tie one end of the cord to each hole.

Monkey

1 Hold a paper plate to your face. Have an adult draw around where your eyes and mouth are. Have an adult help cut out the eye and mouth holes.

2 Paint the mask tan. Paint the rim of the plate brown. Paint a brown point down from the rim above the eyes. Outline the eyes with brown paint.

3 Paint a brown circle around the mouth Outline the mouth with pink paint. Paint two small, black ovals for the **nostrils**.

4 Use brown foam or construction paper for the ears. Cut out two circles. **Staple** the ears to the sides of the plate.

5 Have an adult cut a **slot** in the rim of the plate under the mouth. Slide a paint stirring stick into the slot. Tape the stick to the back of the plate. Use the stick to hold the mask in front of your face.

Furry Monster

This cute mask will make your friends giggle.

Supply List
- thick paper plate
- pencil
- scissors
- purple acrylic paint
- paintbrush
- small Styrofoam balls
- furry fabric
- glue
- hole punch
- 2 pipe cleaners
- elastic cord

1. Hold a paper plate to your face. Have an adult draw around where your eyes and mouth are. Have an adult help cut out the eye and mouth holes.

2. Paint the plate and two Styrofoam balls purple. Let the paint dry.

3. Make eyebrows and cheeks out of the furry **fabric**. Cut thick and wide eyebrows. Use circles for the cheeks. Glue them onto the plate.

4. Punch two holes at the top of the plate. Push the end of a pipe cleaner into each ball. Stick the other ends of the pipe cleaners into the holes. Bend each pipe cleaner and twist it around itself.

5. Punch a hole on each side of the plate. Cut a piece of elastic cord. It should reach around the back of your head. Tie one end of the cord to each hole.

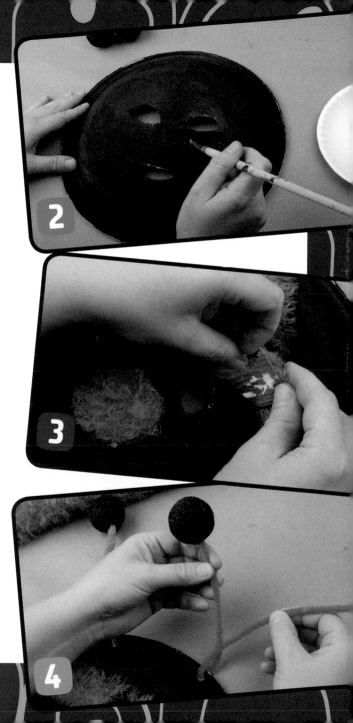

Buzz Buzz Fly

Buzz around in this funny fly mask!

Supply List

- egg carton
- scissors
- hole punch
- green acrylic paint
- paintbrush
- small Styrofoam balls
- glue
- sequins
- 1 red and 2 green pipe cleaners
- elastic cord

1. Cut out two cups from an egg carton. Leave the cups connected to each other.

2. Hold the cups with the bottoms facing towards you. Use a hole punch to make a hole on the upper side of each cup. Then punch holes on the **outer** sides of the cups.

3. Punch a hole between the cups.

4. Have an adult help you cut a hole in the bottom of each cup. These are the eye holes. They should be a little bigger than the hole punch holes.

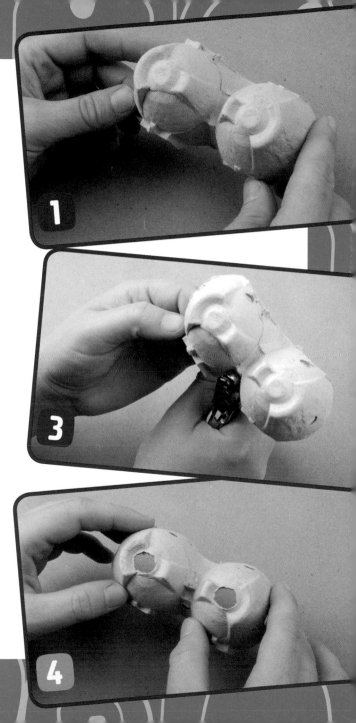

13

5 Paint the cups and the Styrofoam balls green. Let the paint dry.

6 Cover the cups with glue. Add the sequins. Start by putting sequins in a circle around each eye hole.

7 Keep adding sequins in bigger circles as you go around the cups. Cover the cups with sequins. Be careful not to cover up the eye holes. Let the glue dry.

8 Push a green pipe cleaner into each Styrofoam ball. These are the antennae.

9 Connect the antennae to the top holes of the cups. Push a pipe cleaner through each hole. Bend each pipe cleaner and twist it around itself.

10 Roll the red pipe cleaner into a **coil**. Leave one end straight. Connect the straight end to the hole between the cups. This is the fly's mouth.

11 Cut a piece of elastic cord. It should reach around the back of your head. Tie one end of the cord to each of the side holes.

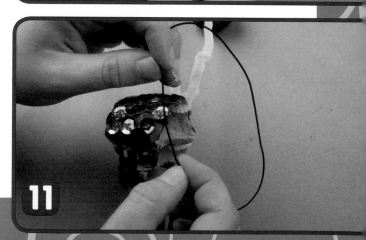

Fun Foam Masks

These colorful masks will surprise and delight your friends!

Alien

1 Set the plastic party mask on a sheet of craft foam. Trace around the bottom of the mask. Make the forehead of the mask a lot taller. Trace the eye holes too.

2 Cut out the mask. To cut the eye holes, bend the foam gently. Make a small cut in the middle of each eye. Then cut along the outline of the eye holes.

3 Outline the eyes with a black marker. Glue on a bunch of googly eyes. Put them wherever you want.

4 Paint the Styrofoam balls. Push a pipe cleaner into each ball. Poke the other ends through the mask. Bend each pipe cleaner and twist it around itself.

5 Cut a piece of elastic cord. It should reach around the back of your head. **Staple** the ends of the cord to the back of the mask near the eye holes.

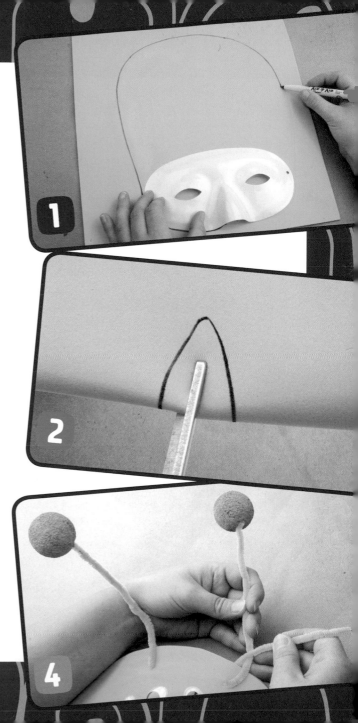

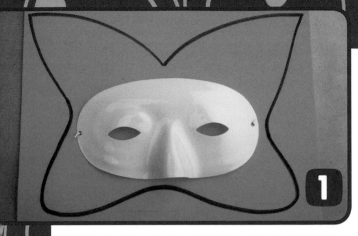

Butterfly

1 Draw the shape of butterfly wings on a piece of foam. Make it taller and wider than the party mask.

2 Set the party mask inside the wings and trace the eye holes.

3 Cut out the wings and the eye holes.

4 On another piece of foam draw the butterfly's body and head. This piece should be as tall as the wings. Cut out the body and head shape. Glue it in the middle of the wings.

5 Decorate the butterfly wings with foam shapes. Glue googly eyes onto the butterfly's head.

6 Cut a piece of elastic cord. It should reach around the back of your head. **Staple** the ends of the cord to the back of the mask near the eye holes.

More Super Ideas

Try making other animals.

lizard

bee

bird

Felt Party Mask

Some felt and glue will make the coolest party mask!

1. Draw a fun mask shape on a piece of felt. It should be a little bigger than the plastic party mask.

2. Put the plastic party mask inside the shape. Trace the eye holes onto the felt. Or try drawing your own shapes for eye holes.

3. Cut out the mask and the eye holes. Make a hole on each side with a hole punch.

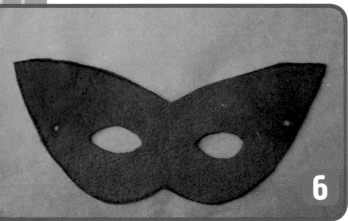

4. In a bucket, mix ½ cup of glue with ½ cup of water.

5. Put your felt mask shape in the **mixture**. Let it **soak** for 10 minutes.

6. Lay the felt on a piece of wax paper to dry. It will get stiff as it dries.

7. When the mask is dry, decorate it! Outline the eye holes with glitter glue. You can glue on feathers or sequins.

8. Cut a piece of elastic cord. It should reach around the back of your head. Tie one end of the cord to each of the side holes.

More Super Ideas

Try these animal shapes.

cat

mouse

tiger

Wacky Bags

Turn plain bags into weird and wacky masks!

Supply List

- paper bag
- acrylic paint
- paintbrush
- marker
- scissors
- silver cupcake liners
- glue
- aluminum foil
- pipe cleaners
- duct tape
- paper streamers
- yarn
- construction paper

Robot

1. Find a paper bag that fits over your head. It should cover your face, but not touch your shoulders. You may need to make it shorter.

2. Paint the front of the bag gray. Let the paint dry.

3. Put the bag over your head. Ask an adult to mark where your eyes and mouth are.

4. Take the bag off. Draw circles for the eyes and a rectangle for the mouth. Cut out the eyes and mouth.

5. Glue silver cupcake liners onto the bag in rows. The liners should **overlap**. Cut liners in half to cover small areas.

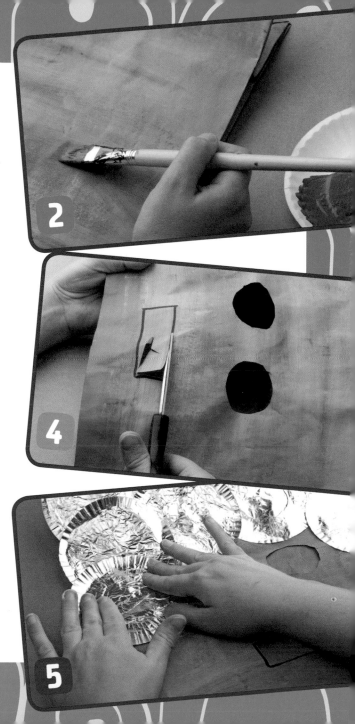

6 Cut out the centers of two liners and glue them around the eye holes.

7 Cut off the edges of any cupcake liners that hang off the side of the bag.

8 Make two balls of aluminum foil and wrap them around pipe cleaners. Push the ends of the pipe cleaners through the top of the bag.

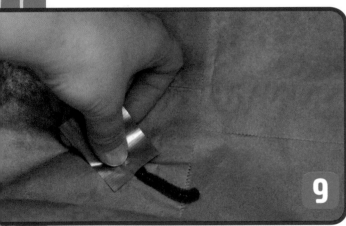

9 Reach inside the bag and fold the ends of the pipe cleaners. Tape the ends to the inside of the bag.

10 Twist other pipe cleaners into **spirals.** Glue them onto the bag for decoration.

Swamp Monster

1. Find a paper bag that fits over your head. It should cover your face, but not touch your shoulders. You may need to make it shorter.

2. Paint the front of the bag blue. Let the paint dry.

3. Put the bag over your head. Ask an adult to mark where your eyes and mouth are. Cut out squares for the eyes and a squiggly oval for the mouth.

4. Cut long pieces of yarn and paper streamers. Glue them around the top of the bag. Make it look like messy hair.

5. Cut a tongue out of construction paper. Make sure it is narrower than the mouth hole. Fold the end of the tongue. Put it through the mouth hole. Tape it to the inside of the mask.

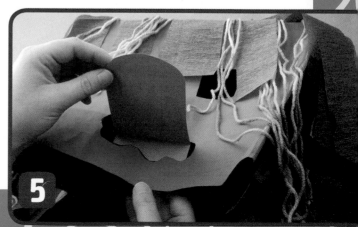

Colorful Faces

Create a fun new face!

Supply List
- poster board
- pencil
- scissors
- glue
- acrylic paint
- paintbrush
- construction paper
- stapler
- elastic cord

1. Fold a rectangular piece of poster board in half. Draw a half circle from one end of the folded side to the other.

2. Cut along the line. When you unfold the poster board you will have an oval shape.

3. Hold the oval up to your face. Ask an adult to mark where your eyes are. Draw and cut out eye holes.

4. Cut a triangle out of poster board for the nose. Fold it in half. Unfold it part way and glue the sides to the mask. The nose should stick out a little. Press firmly and hold until the glue sets.

5. Paint the mask. You can use just one color, or paint stripes or another **design**. Let the paint dry.

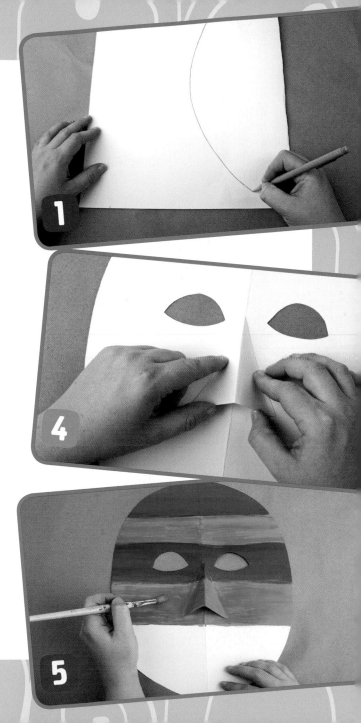

6 Decorate your mask with construction paper shapes. Try folding strips of construction paper to make curly hair.

7 Make 1-inch (3-cm) cuts along the fold at the bottom and the top of the mask.

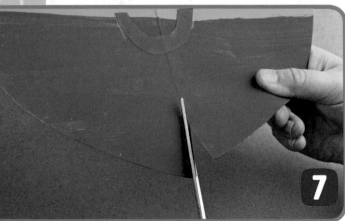

8 Fold the mask slightly so that the edges of the top cut **overlap**. **Staple** the edges of the cut together. Do the same thing for the bottom cut.

9 Cut a piece of elastic cord. It should reach around the back of your head. Staple the ends of the cord to the sides of the mask.

More Super Ideas

Experiment using different materials.

Glossary

coil – a spiral or a series of loops.

design – a decorative pattern or arrangement.

fabric – woven material or cloth.

mixture – a combination of two or more different things.

nostril – an opening in the nose.

outer – on the outside.

overlap – to lie partly on top of something.

project – a task or activity.

slot – a narrow opening.

soak – to leave something in a liquid for awhile.

spiral – a pattern that winds in a circle.

staple – to use a stapler to fasten something together with a thin wire.

whisker – one of the long hairs around the mouth of an animal.

About SUPER SANDCASTLE™

Bigger Books for Emerging Readers
Grades K–4

Created for library, classroom, and at-home use, Super SandCastle™ books support and engage young readers as they develop and build literacy skills and will increase their general knowledge about the world around them. Super SandCastle™ books are an extension of SandCastle™, the leading preK–3 imprint for emerging and beginning readers. Super SandCastle™ features a larger trim size for more reading fun.

Let Us Know

Super SandCastle™ would like to hear your stories about reading this book. What was your favorite page? Was there something hard that you needed help with? Share the ups and downs of learning to read. We want to hear from you! Send us an e-mail.

sandcastle@abdopublishing.com

Contact us for a complete list of SandCastle™, Super SandCastle™, and other nonfiction and fiction titles from ABDO Publishing Company.

www.abdopublishing.com • 8000 West 78th Street
Edina, MN 55439 • 800-800-1312 • 952-831-1632 fax